In the Dark

Written by Claire Llewellyn

Illustrated by Karen Oppatt

Collins

It is dark.

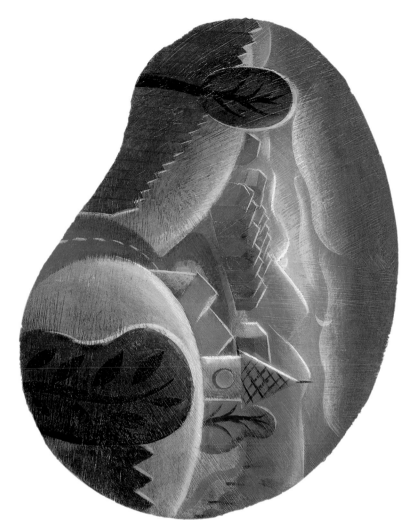

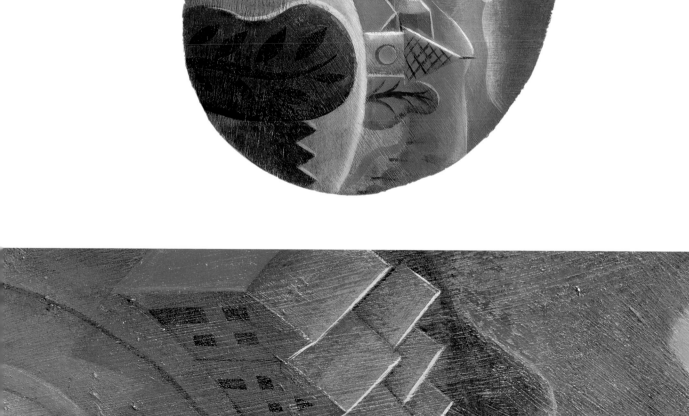

It is dark in the park.

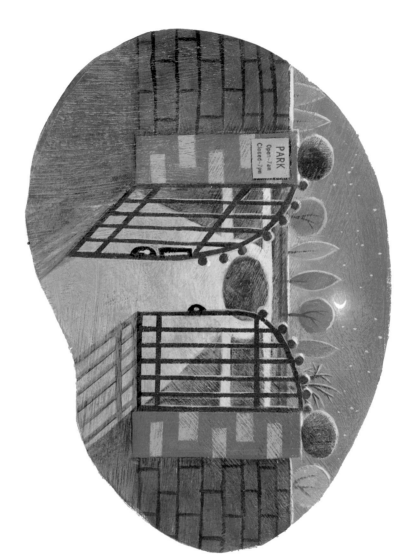

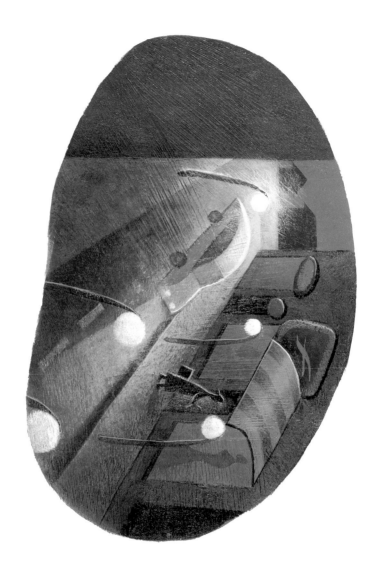 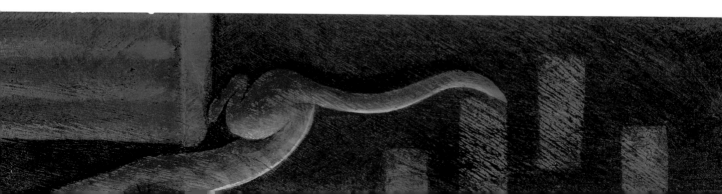

6

It is dark in the street.

It is dark in the city.

It is dark in the wood.

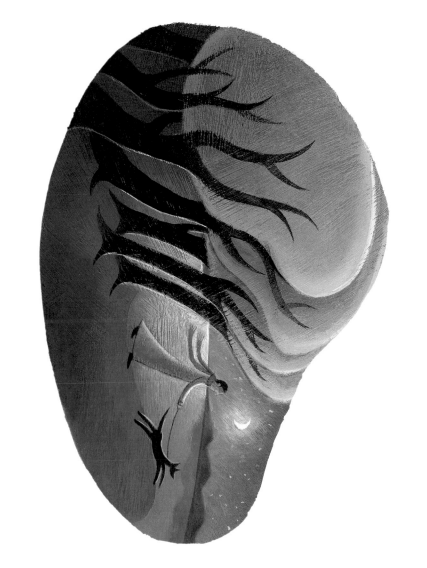

It is dark at home.

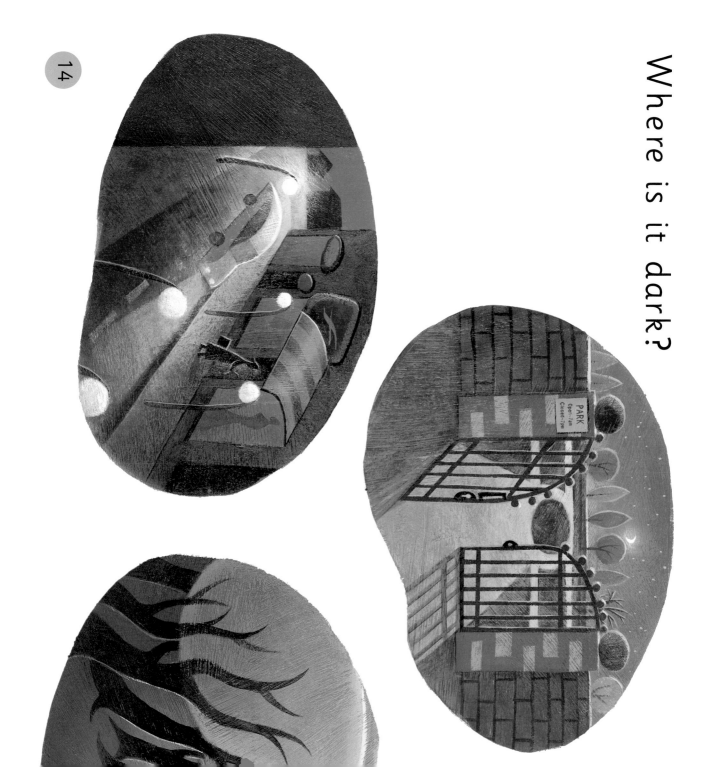

Where is it dark?

Ideas for guided reading

Learning objectives: understanding and using terms about books and print: book, cover, author, illustration, word, letter, title; matching spoken and written words; hearing and saying initial phonemes in words; asking and answering questions and offering suggestions

Curriculum links: Knowledge and understanding of the world (features of the natural world; asking questions about why things happen)

High frequency words: it, is, in, the

Interest words: dark, park, street, city, wood, home

Word count: 36

Resources: Thick paper, wax crayons, dark blue ink

Getting started

- Ask the children to look carefully at the front cover. How many words are there in the title? Point at each word and read. Encourage the children to use the correct terms 'title' and 'cover'.

- Walk through the book to p13 and look at the pictures. Ask the children to name each place as you go e.g. *park, city, wood.*

- Ask the children to point to the word *dark* on each page. What sound or letter does it start with?

- Ask the children which words are repeated on each page after p4, i.e. 'It is dark in the'. Model one-to-one matching, pointing at each word.

Reading and responding

- Ask the children to read the book independently from the beginning. As the children read, prompt and praise correct matching of spoken and written words. Prompt the children to use a variety of cues including initial sounds to read unfamiliar words.

- Prompt correct page turning, and left-right direction.